Bridging the Gap
*Mindful Intergenerational
Connections*

Table of Contents

Chapter 1. Introduction

Experience the joy of connection like never before in our Special Report, "Bridging the Gap: Mindful Intergenerational Connections!" Revealing a path strewn with delightful insights, this report unravels the rewarding process of forming deep, purposeful links between different generations. Be prepared to embark on a journey, exploring how mindfulness paves the way for understanding, empathy, and a shared narrative across the age spectrum. Bursting with practical advice, powerful real-life examples, and cutting-edge research, this report promises to guide families, communities, and organizations towards a more harmonious, interconnected future. Seize this rare opportunity to deepen your relationships and celebrate a meaningful exchange of wisdom and experiences. Order your copy today, and begin to bridge the gap!

Chapter 2. Bridging the Ages: An Introduction

The pace at which our world advances technologically is a marvel, a testament to human innovation and creativity. Yet, the rapidity of these changes sometimes inadvertently draws deep trenches between generations, setting them apart like disparate islands in the sea of time. But if one were to leap over the gap and bridge these islands, there lies an enriching amalgamation - a blending of experiences, wisdom and knowledge that not only binds us as a collective body but also illuminates our individual paths in life. In this chapter, we explore the avenues that facilitate these intergenerational connections, investigate the benefits that they deliver, and elucidate how they foster rich personal growth and societal synergy.

2.1. The Significance of Intergenerational Connections

Intergenerational connections represent a thriving conduit for communication, appreciation, and mutual respect between younger and older generations. Fortified by shared narratives, a common heritage, and exchange of experiences, these ties often form the cornerstone of diverse societies around the world.

Engaging in intergenerational relationships exposes one to a breadth of perspectives, allowing for an enriched understanding of the world around us. History is enlivened through the personal accounts of older generations, while the newer generations harness the power of innovation and fresh perspectives, shaping the future.

The contrast between generations is not a chasm to separate, but a spectrum of experiences that provide a profound insight into the trajectory of human civilization. It is imperative that we recognize the need to cultivate these connections and instill a culture of communication, respect, and empathy between different age groups.

2.2. The Power of Mindfulness in Fostering Connections

Mindfulness, in essence, is the practice of being fully present, engaged, and responsive in one's immediate experience. The application of mindfulness in fostering intergenerational relationships is expansive and impactful. By focusing on the present, individuals encourage genuine conversations, fostering trust, understanding, and robust exchange of ideas.

By promoting empathy and understanding through shared narratives, mindfulness becomes a potent tool in bridging the generational divide and cultivating stronger familial, social, and community bonds, thereby fostering a society enriched by collective wisdom.

2.3. The Challenges and Solutions in Bridging Generations

While the importance of fostering these connections is well-established, it's critical to recognize the obstacles that may stand in the way. The varying pace of life, differing communication styles, and contrasting worldviews between generations could pose challenges to forming connections.

Tech-aided communication, a mainstay of young generations, may be a hurdle for older generations. Similarly, younger generations might struggle with older communication styles. Recognizing these barriers and employing empathy, patience, and creativity can help overcome them, fostering rewarding relationships. Regular conversations, shared activities promoting mutual growth, and utilizing common interests as ice-breakers, can successfully foster connection and understanding across generations.

To bridge the gap, it requires conscious effort, an embrace of mutual respect, a willingness to communicate, and an acceptance of differing perspectives. As such, it becomes a journey of self-growth, mutual understanding, and building stronger communities interconnected through shared wisdom and diverse experience.

2.4. Harnessing the Benefits: The Symbiotic Exchange

Intergenerational connections create a symbiotic exchange of knowledge, understanding, and support. While older generations convey hard-earned wisdom, life experience, and lessons learned to the younger generations, the younger cohorts offer freshness of perspective, innovation, and an understanding of the modern world.

In practical terms, this might mean mentor-mentee relationships, apprenticeship programs, or interactive community projects that allow active learning and mutual respect to flourish. This exchange becomes a two-way street, paving the way for societal harmony and collaborative growth.

2.5. A More Harmonious Future: The Societal Impact

The societal implications of a stronger intergenerational fabric are vast. Empathy across age spectrums can result in more inclusive policies, mutual support systems, and community harmony, amongst others. The shared narrative of mutual respect, empathy, and reciprocity can even promote more inclusive environments, helping societies tackle larger issues like discrimination, ageism, and social exclusion.

In conclusion, bridging the generational gaps involves not just the forging of relationships, but the mindful cultivation of these ties. As these connections flourish, they create a tapestry of shared experiences and wisdom that enrich personhood and strengthen societal links. By engaging mindfully and empathetically with different generations, we unlock a more inclusive, connected, and harmonious future - a legacy for generations to come.

Chapter 3. Understanding Generational Differences

In the quest to form enduring, harmonious relationships with different generations, recognizing and comprehending generational differences is an indispensable first step. These differences, often borne out of unique historical, societal, and personal contexts, play a significant role in shaping individuals' outlooks, value systems, and modes of communication.

3.1. Understanding the Generational Spectrum

Numerous studies have segmented modern society into various generations, each exhibiting their own distinctive characteristics. Each segment—distinguished by different influences, experiences, attitudes, and behaviors—adds nuanced variety to our complex societal tapestry. The widely recognized generational categories include:

- Traditionalists or the Silent Generation (1927–1945),

- Baby Boomers (1946–1964),

- Generation X (1965–1980),

- Millennials or Generation Y (1981–1996),

- and the emerging Generation Z (1997–2012).

This understanding, though simplified, provides a broad framework for understanding generational differences. It is essential to remember that individual traits may diverge from their generational archetype.

3.2. Decoding the Generational Code

Going beyond labelling, it is crucial to comprehend each of these generation's distinctive influences, values, and socio-political contexts to strengthen intergenerational connections.

Born between 1927 to 1945, Traditionalists grew up amid significant events, including World War II and the Great Depression, which imprinted a strong sense of stability, order, and obedience on their psyches. They value respect for authority and collective security and appreciate face-to-face communication.

On the other hand, Baby Boomers, fuelled by unprecedented post-war economic prosperity, adopted liberal, optimistic, and individualistic views. They possessed a strong work ethic and proved themselves to be innovative thinkers.

Generation X, coming after the Boomers, grew up during a time of societal change and technological advancement, fostering a blend of traditionalist loyalty and millennial innovativeness. Often noted for their independence and pragmatism, this generation is considered adaptable and resourceful.

Millennials came of age in the fast-paced world of the internet and social media. They're globally conscious, tech-savvy, and appreciate flexible working structures. They're known for their multitasking abilities and seeking personal fulfillment and purpose in their occupations.

In the Gen Z cohort, digital technology has been woven into their lives from birth, fostering an intuitiveness about digital communication. They tend to be pragmatic and anxious, concerned about their economic future.

3.3. Respect in Communication

Every generation's communication preferences are informed by their upbringing and the technological environment they grew up in. Traditionalists and Baby Boomers typically prefer face-to-face or telephone communication, while Gen Xers might opt for email. Millennials and Gen Z, with the world at their fingertips, are comfortable across multiple platforms, from social media to instant messaging and video conferencing.

Understanding these preferences paves the way to effective conversations and meaningful connections. Remember, respect is the key, acknowledging one's preferred communication mode conveys respect for their comfort and personality.

3.4. Navigating Values and Motivations

Similar to communication styles, each generation has unique motivations that influence their priorities and behaviours. Acknowledging and appreciating these differences can help avoid misunderstandings, build empathy, and foster harmonious relationships.

For example, Traditionalists, having witnessed extreme hardships, may value financial security above all, while the Baby Boomers, having grown in a comparatively prosperous era, might value self-realization more. This can sometimes lead to a clash of viewpoints, but it's essential to remember that different perspectives are not inherently wrong, but a result of diverse experiences.

3.5. Bridging the Gap with Respect and Empathy

Recognizing generational differences is not an end in itself but a means to build bridges of understanding, respect, and empathy among different age groups. Openness to diverse perspectives, mutual respect for individual experiences, and the willingness to adapt our communication styles can go a long way in making meaningful intergenerational connections.

Through understanding, we pave the way to harmony, learning to accept and value the unique stories, skills, and experiences each generation offers. This acceptance forms the foundation for diverse, interactive communities, where wisdom and vibrancy mingle, creating inclusive spaces that embrace and celebrate generational diversity.

Chapter 4. Mindfulness: The Powerful Bridge

Our journey begins with an exploration of mindfulness, a wonderful tool to connect, communicate and establish deeper relationships among different generations.

Mindfulness, at its most basic, is the practice of being present in the moment, focusing completely on one task or experience at a time, and accepting it wholly without judgment. It might appear to be a simple concept, yet it has profound implications on our daily living, relationships, and our perception of the world around us.

4.1. The Foundation of Mindfulness

Mindfulness enables us to pay closer attention to our own emotional responses and cues from those around us. Through heightened self-awareness and emotional intelligence, we can ensure more authentic, fulfilling interactions with others.

Research shows that mindfulness has its roots in ancient meditative practices, particularly those within the Buddhist tradition. Mindfulness, however, is not solely a religious or spiritual practice. There is an increasing understanding today of mindfulness as a powerful psychological tool with profound implications for mental and emotional well-being.

To practice mindfulness, you must first learn to stay present in the moment. This requires constant reminding to let go of fretting about the past or worrying about the future. No daydreaming, zoning out, or scrolling through your phone. Just undivided attention to the task at hand, and acceptance of your thoughts and emotions as they arise.

4.2. A Deeper Connection Through Mindfulness

When mindfulness is exercised in interpersonal relationships, it can foster more profound bonds and understanding. It allows us to go beyond surface-level interactions and dive into deeper layers of connection.

Imagine a dialogue where each person actively listens, stays wholly present, and responds thoughtfully without hasty judgment. Both parties feel understood and valued in such a discourse, paving the way for a more genuine connection. This is what mindfulness can bring about in communication, thereby transforming relationships.

It isn't always easy to practice this level of mindfulness, particularly when conversing across generational divides. Different worldviews, experiences, and technological competence can create substantial gaps in understanding. However, mindfulness can help bridge these gaps by fostering an environment of patience, empathy, and non-judgmental listening.

4.3. Mindfulness: Bridging Generational Gaps

Intergenerational communication is often fraught with stereotypes, prejudices, and misunderstandings. This is where mindfulness can play a significant role in bridging the divide.

When you approach an intergenerational dialogue mindfully, you dedicate your entire focus to truly understanding the other person's perspective without any predetermined notions. You see beyond surface-level age-related stereotypes and biases, and instead, you perceive the individual's character, experiences, and wisdom.

By being mindful, we tend to ask more open-ended questions and listen more actively. This open communication fosters a higher level of respect and appreciation, bolstering the bond between generations.

Take, for instance, a conversation between a grandparent and grandchild. Typically, they converse from entirely different life perspectives. However, with mindfulness, the grandparent can better understand the grandchild's world – the trials, tribulations, aspirations of growing up in a world driven by technology and rapid change. Simultaneously, the grandchild gains a newfound appreciation for the grandparent's experiences and wisdom, fostering a rich exchange of not just words but values, ideals, and understandings.

4.4. The Power of Mindfulness in Practice

According to a study by Brown et al. (2007), individuals who reported higher levels of mindfulness were more satisfied in their relationships. They were better able to respond to relationship stress, communicate their emotions, and were less moody.

Furthermore, another study by Barnes et al. (2007) revealed that in families practicing mindfulness techniques, there was a decrease in perceived stress and an improvement in overall well-being. Clearly, the impact of mindfulness extends well beyond the individual, positively affecting families, communities, and subsequently entire generations.

Mindfulness in an organizational setup, too, has proven to increase well-being and productivity. It is now incorporated into training modules by many progressive businesses to foster a culture of connection, collaboration, and sustained focus.

Indeed, mindfulness has the power to bridge generational gaps and create synergistic relationships. It is the thread that can weave a more harmonious, connected world, inspiring a shared narrative across different age groups.

Harnessing mindfulness should not be a sporadic effort but rather a daily commitment. Like any useful skill, mindfulness improves with practice, and its effects are increasingly felt and observed over time.

This journey of mindfulness will undoubtedly have challenges, but the rewards it brings in improved relationships, inner peace, and a more empathetic society make the endeavor worthwhile. So let's embark on this journey together, exploring and establishing mindful intergenerational connections that are deeper, more meaningful, and that bridge the divide we often assume to be insurmountable.

Chapter 5. The Art of Active Listening Across Generations

Active listening is often touted as an effective interaction strategy. It is the practice of fully engaging and concentrating on the speaker and their message, not just hearing but understanding the content, context, and emotions latent within their words. In the context of intergenerational communication, it serves as a potent tool to bridge the gaps of age, experiences, and perspectives. However, mastering the art of active listening involves more than just staying quiet while another person speaks. It necessitates a deep sense of empathy and mindfulness that unveils layers of meaning beneath the spoken words.

5.1. Emphasizing Empathy and Authenticity

Active listening can only be genuinely accomplished when it is underpinned by true empathy and authenticity. Empathy allows us to understand and share the feelings of others, thereby promoting connection. Authenticity keeps us grounded and honest in our interactions, which fosters trust and openness.

The art of active listening becomes more nuanced when practiced between generations. Every generation has its unique experiences, perspectives, and knowledge, which can contribute to making communication complex yet enriching.

5.2. Role of Non-Verbal Cues

Non-verbal cues play just as crucial a role in communication as verbal communication. Understanding this importance will augment our active listening skills. Observing the speaker's body language, facial expressions, and other non-verbal signs can provide invaluable insights into their emotions and perspectives. For example, a grandparent's gentle nod when recounting their past might indicate agreement or affirmation of their experiences, while crossed arms might suggest defensiveness or discomfort.

Active listeners also need to become adept at using non-verbal cues themselves. It might involve conveying interest through nodding affirmatively, maintaining eye contact, offering a gentle touch or pat, or positioning your body to face the speaker, all signs that you are engaged and respectful of the speaker's narrative.

5.3. Exercise Mindfulness

Mindfulness involves keeping our focus in the moment and being completely present. It plays a significant role in fostering active listening skills across generations. With mindfulness, we consciously put aside our preconceived notions or judgments about the other person's experiences and opinions. By staying present in the conversation, we allow ourselves the space to understand their narrative authentically.

Mindfulness also involves self-awareness, where we grow conscious of our own reactions, offering us the opportunity to control our responses, encourage a positive exchange, and avoid negative triggers.

5.4. Dealing with Distractions

Distractions ease their way subtly during a conversation and may hinder the practice of active listening. This could range from technological distractions, such as incoming emails or social media notifications, to mental diversions, such as being consumed by your own thoughts or prejudiced ideas regarding the speaker's words.

Active listening requires overcoming these impediments by creating a conducive environment for conversation and disciplining our minds to focus.

5.5. Communicating Across Language Barriers

Language usage and comprehension largely differ across generations, which can pose a communication challenge. Terms, phrases, and idioms popular in one era might be unfamiliar to another. Active listeners maintain a mindset of curiosity and openness, navigating these barriers with gentle questions to understand the speaker better and respond appropriately.

5.6. Narrative and Storytelling

Narrative and storytelling are powerful tools to share experiences and wisdom across generations. Encouraging the speaker to share stories from their life not only stirs their memory and interest but also provides you with a rich tapestry of experiences to understand their perspectives better. This approach also encourages empathy and forms bonds that help deepen intergenerational relationships.

5.7. Applying Active Listening in Everyday Life

Possessing theoretical knowledge about active listening is one thing, but applying it in everyday life is what truly counts. Whether listening to a grandparent's anecdote, a parent's advice, or a young child's recounting of their day at school, the principles of active listening can be used to establish stronger, more meaningful connections.

In the end, the art of active listening strives to transform casual conversations into meaningful exchanges across age groups. As we listen actively and grow to understand each other, we cherish the shared narrative that weaves together the diverse threads of our experiences. The wisdom of the old, the energy of the young, and the knowledge exchange resulting from active listening creates a harmonious, interconnected world, one conversation at a time.

Chapter 6. Unlocking Empathy Towards different Age Groups

In an era of rapid technological development and an accelerated pace of life, it can be easy to overlook the importance of nurturing close connections with individuals from diverse age groups. However, fostering these relationships can be immensely rewarding, offering experiences steeped in shared wisdom, exchanged stories, and mutual growth. Empathy, particularly intergenerational empathy, plays a pivotal role in building these bridges of understanding. Throughout this chapter, we examine the importance of unlocking empathy toward different age groups, the practical methods of developing it, and the transformative effects it can have on personal and societal scales.

6.1. The Power of Empathy

Empathy—the capability to comprehend and share others' feelings—is a profound human trait that enables us to form emotional bonds, enabling us to understand and relate to the feelings of people around us. It allows us to resonate empathically with experiences outside our own and fosters relationships rich in mutual respect and understanding.

Unlocking empathy towards different age groups paves the path for creating a society that respects, values, and learns from everyone regardless of their age. It fosters intergenerational relationships that debunk stereotypes, redefine understanding, and foster an environment of acceptance and growth. It helps younger generations realize the wisdom and experienced learned from life's ups and downs, while helping older people understand the freshness, enthusiasm, and creative thinking of younger individuals.

6.2. Breaking Stereotypes and Bias

Quite often, age-related stereotypes and biases obstruct our ability to empathize fully with different age groups. These prejudices can emerge from various sources such as the media, social circles, culture, or even past experiences. Recognizing these biases and making a conscious effort to dismiss them is the first step in creating meaningful intergenerational connections.

Consider starting with open conversations or constructive dialogues about age-related stereotypes in safe, inclusive environments. These discussions can help individuals be more aware of their perceptions and preconceived notions, thereby encouraging them to confront and reassess these biases.

6.3. Practical Exercises for Developing Empathy

The cultivation of empathy is analogous to developing a muscle; it requires consistent practice and effort. Various strategies can facilitate increased empathy towards different age groups.

Exercises such as role-playing can help individuals step into the shoes of another age group, experiencing the world from their perspective. Regular interactions with diverse age groups, in the form of community gatherings or family meet-ups, also enhances empathy. Reading literature or watching films that portray the experiences of different age groups is another effective way to understand and empathize with their perspectives.

+ Multigenerational interactions: Regularly interacting with people from varied age groups broadens your perspective and challenges you to understand their experiences and viewpoints.

+ Act of listening: Active listening is a critical part of empathy. By paying full attention to what others are saying and expressing, we can better appreciate their feelings and thoughts.

+ Expressing empathy: It is important to not just understand the feelings and perspectives of others, but to also communicate this understanding back to them. This validates their feelings and ends up creating a stronger bond.

6.4. Empathy in Action: Case Studies

To underscore the transformative power of empathy, let's consider a couple of real-life examples. In 'A Place for Us' - an innovative housing project in Cleveland, residents ranging from students to seniors live together under one roof, participating in scheduled interactions. This project has paved the way for remarkable connections and taught valuable lessons about unity in diversity, breaking age-based stereotypes.

Another notable initiative is the United Kingdom's 'Chatback' program, an intergenerational theatre project that brings together teenagers and seniors to create productions based on their life stories. The project has shown remarkable success, portraying the generational divide as a transformative and creative force rather than a barrier, reinforcing the power of empathy in bridging age gaps.

6.5. The Ripple Effects of Empathy

Empathy toward different age groups does not just enrich personal relationships; it has far-reaching implications in various fields—from education and healthcare to corporate cultures and community building. It encourages policies that promote inclusivity and respect, reshaping societal structures into more caring, kindness-oriented groups.

In education, adopting an empathetic approach can enhance teaching methods and create more supportive learning environments. In healthcare, it helps in developing patient-centric care models. In workplaces, empathy fosters an accepting culture, boosting collaboration, and innovation across different age groups.

In conclusion, empathy—the ability to understand and share the feelings of others—is a cornerstone of harmonious intergenerational relationships. The path to unlocking empathy involves practicing conscious understanding, breaking down stereotypes, and active listening. While this journey requires effort, the rewards of connecting deeply with people from diverse age groups make it a journey worth embarking on.

Chapter 7. Practical Techniques for Facilitating Connection

Forming real and lasting connections across different generations is both a rewarding and challenging task. However, with practical techniques and guided approaches, compelling intergenerational relationships can be formed, leading to exchange of wisdom and enriching experiences. This chapter lays out a step-by-step guide comprising techniques and strategies for facilitating meaningful intergenerational connections.

7.1. Opening the Dialogue

Facilitating a connection begins with opening a dialogue. It's essential to create a safe space that invites open interaction and sharing of experiences. Setting up a comfortable environment can involve organizing meet-ups in familiar settings or arranging virtual meetings to bridge physical distances. Utilizing simple icebreaker activities can also be beneficial in easing the participants into the conversation.

7.2. Practicing Active Listening

Active listening is a powerful technique to foster strong interpersonal relationships. It allows individuals to understand and absorb the other person's experiences, thereby paving the path for empathy. Teaching the younger generation about the importance of active listening and enabling them with tools like summarizing, paraphrasing, and showing non-verbal cues of understanding, will foster enduring connections.

7.3. Storytelling: A Powerful Connection Tool

The innate human fascination with stories makes this a compelling tool for connection. Encourage the older generation to share their life experiences in the form of stories— their triumphs, trials, lessons, and life decisions. Simultaneously, ask the younger generation to share their aspirations, challenges, and experiences. Recognize and respect the unique perspectives shared through these narratives to cultivate mutual understanding.

7.4. Practicing Empathy: Walking in Another's Shoes

Practicing empathy, understanding and sharing the feelings of another, is a pivotal step towards forming a deep connection. It requires effort, tenacity and cognizance to perceive the world from another's point of view. Integrating role-play activities or guided discussions featuring hypothetical scenarios can aid in developing empathy.

7.5. Using Technology to Bridge Distances

With the advent of technology, physical distances are no longer a hurdle for interaction. Planning virtual meet-ups, or creating a common platform to share experiences and ideas can ensure uninterrupted connection. Simultaneously, one of the key challenges can be to bridge the technology gap between generations. Providing tech literacy to the elders will be a step towards overcoming this barrier.

7.6. Introducing Reciprocal Teaching

The concept of reciprocal teaching involves two-way sharing of knowledge. It encourages the participants to grasp new ideas or competencies from each other. The older generation could impart wisdom through their rich experiences, while youngsters can educate elders about new technological advancements or contemporary ideas. This can enhance mutual respect and admiration, making way for stronger connections.

7.7. Engaging in Shared Activities

Engaging in common hobbies or shared activities can create bonding experiences. These could range from cooking, gardening, art, or even participating in community services. Such shared experiences reinforce mutual understanding and build shared narratives, thereby fostering the desired connections.

7.8. Handling Differences: Conflict Resolution

Conflicts and disagreements are integral to any relationship. Teaching conflict resolution techniques like open communication, constructive criticism, avoidance of blame game, and decision making through consensus, can help navigate these differences smoothly, and make way for stronger relationships in the long run.

7.9. Encouraging Regular Interaction

The virtue of persistence cannot be overstated when fostering intergenerational connections. Regular interaction not only allows recognition and appreciation of the evolving dynamics of the relationship, but also strengthens the bond over time.

The path to creating intergenerational connections might be laden with efforts and challenges, but the rewards it brings are colossal. By implementing these practical techniques, and tailoring them according to specific needs and dynamics, one can create a harmonious canvas of rich experiences and enduring friendships across generations. It is an investment of time and patience that pays off with profound connection, shared wisdom, and a delightful interplay of varied perspectives.

Chapter 8. Case Studies: Success Stories of Intergenerational Bonding

One cannot fully comprehend the profound impact of intergenerational bonds without witnessing its manifestation in real-life situations. Hence, this section is dedicated to success stories that illustrate the effectiveness and rich layers of these precious connections.

8.1. The Tale of Young Jason and Mr. Murray

Jason, an avid tech enthusiast, decided to volunteer at Evergreen Care Facility as a part of his school's community service initiative. Mr. Murray, an 80-year-old resident at Evergreen, always had a deep-seated interest in computers but had never had an opportunity to unravel the mysteries of technology.

Jason began teaching Mr. Murray the ropes: from turning on a computer to browsing the Internet, sending emails, and video conferencing. The learning process, though slow at first, became more fluid over time. These sessions became the highlight of their week. They shared laughter, frustration, victories, and an ever-growing bond.

It was not just Mr. Murray who benefited. Jason found great satisfaction in teaching and helping someone learn a new skill. Their relationship heralded a wonderful exchange of stories and wisdom, transcending the mere lessons on technology.

8.2. Marilyn and The Smith Family

Marilyn, a retired school teacher, lived alone since she had never married. When the Smiths, a family with two teen-aged children, moved next door, an opportunity for connection emerged.

Initially, it was the usual pleasantries and waves. However, one day, the Smiths urgently needed a babysitter. On a whim, they asked Marilyn, who agreed. She ended up telling the children tales from her childhood and the places she had been. This transformed into regular bedtime storytelling.

Soon, the Smith teens were visiting Marilyn for help with homework, relationship advice, and more. In turn, Marilyn found a new lease of life, having a surrogate family to care and be cared for.

8.3. Organization-level Success: 'Gems of Wisdom' Initiative

An NGO named "Gems of Wisdom", started a meaningful initiative aiming to connect school children with residents in care homes. The idea was simple - the children would interview the elderly residents, collecting stories of their lives. These stories were then showcased on a digital platform.

This started as a project to document history, but soon blossomed into something much bigger. The children formed deep, lasting bonds with the elderly residents, marked by love, respect, and mutual understanding. The residents, in turn, found joy and enthusiasm in their young friends and the fresh perspective they brought. Consequently, this initiative boosted the mental health and well-being of both generations involved.

8.4. Breaking Barriers through Letters

A primary school teacher took a creative approach to instill empathy and respect for elders in her students. She initiated a pen-pal program between her students and a nearby assisted living home. Adolescence involved writing letters, sharing about their lives, and getting advice from their elderly pen pals.

Her students, initially reticent, began looking forward to these letters. There was earnest curiosity about life before iPhones, when people actually wrote letters to each other. Beautiful friendships formed between children and octogenarians, simply with paper and pen.

8.5. A Story of Music

A young musician named Emily offered to perform at a senior living community. The elders were thrilled and appreciated her music greatly. Emily, in turn, was inspired by their stories and wisdom.

One day, Emily met Florence, a retired professional pianist. Florence began giving Emily piano lessons, and their bond strengthened with every chord they struck together. Emily learned music techniques rarely taught nowadays, and Florence found a student eager to learn from her vast experience.

These stories epitomize the power of intergenerational relationships. They demonstrate the value these connections bring, their potential to change lives, and their capacity to bridge generational gaps. While these are just isolated examples, imagine the collective impact of embracing such exchanges as a normative cultural practice. We must endeavor to break down the age barriers, eliminate stereotypes, and build a strong society that respects and values all its members, irrespective of age.

Chapter 9. Challenges in Mindful Intergenerational Connection

While mindfulness can truly lead to transformative intergenerational connections, the path is not without its share of challenges. This chapter delves into some of the most common and significant obstacles that individuals and organizations often grapple with when trying to nurture such bonds.

9.1. The Obstacle of Distinctive Life Experiences

One of the key issues when trying to cultivate mindful intergenerational relationships is dealing with very distinctive life experiences. Each generation comes with its own set of memories, cultural milestones, and historical events that have shaped their worldview. This means that each generation could interpret events, actions, and emotions differently.

For instance, a person from the so-called Silent Generation may have a completely different take on economic thrift or technological engagement compared to a Millennial. Such divergent experiences and subsequent perspectives may lead to misunderstandings and friction. To surmount this hurdle, it is essential to encourage open-minded conversations where these different life experiences are generously shared and respectfully heard.

9.2. Overcoming Differences in Communicative Styles

Another significant hurdle comes in the form of communication style variances across different age groups. Preferred methods of communication differ substantially between generations. While letters and in-person conversations might be the preferred medium of older generations, younger ones may lean towards texting, social media, or video calling.

Awareness of this challenge is the first step towards overcoming it. By recognizing the importance of "meeting in the middle", adopting a hybrid communication approach may prove beneficial for both parties.

9.3. Challenges Stemming from Stereotypes

Stereotypes can force us into cognitive boxes that compartmentalize individuals based on their generational tag. Elders may often be dismissed as old-fashioned, technologically challenged, or conservative, while youths might be labeled as impulsive, tech-obsessed, or reckless. These stereotypes can create barriers and discourage individuals from taking the first step towards fostering intergenerational bonds.

To combat such stereotypes, we need a change of mindset. Cultivating mindfulness can allow us to see beyond these stereotypes, understanding each individual for who they are, rather than the generation they belong to.

9.4. Bridging the Technological Divide

One of the most obvious challenges in forming mindful intergenerational connections is the technological divide. Different levels of comfort, knowledge, and accessibility to technology can prove to be barriers in communication and engagement.

Providing digital literacy support to older adults, along with patience and understanding from younger generations, can make a significant difference in bridging this divide. Additionally, employing a variety of communication methods can also help cater to the comfort levels of all involved parties.

9.5. Navigating Changing Family Structures

Changes in family structures over the years have also contributed to the challenges faced in creating mindful intergenerational bonds. The rise in nuclear family systems and dual-career marriages has increased geographical dispersion and decreased the frequency of interactions across generations.

Creative solutions such as intergeneration-shared living spaces, community events, and designated family time can help circumvent these structural changes.

9.6. Time Constraints

Modern life is often characterized by rushed schedules and high-stress levels, leaving little room for quality family time. Despite the will to cultivate them, mindful intergenerational connections might be sidelined due to time constraints. It is crucial to consciously carve out time for cross-generational interactions to nurture these bonds.

Strengthening intergenerational connections is a worthwhile endeavor that offers numerous benefits. Even though this journey is laden with challenges such as distinctive life experiences, communication style disparities, stereotypes, technological gaps, changing family structures, and time constraints, the rewards of meaningful intergenerational relationships make the effort valuable. Overcoming these barriers requires mindful awareness, open communication, flexibility, and most importantly, time. Remember, this is not a swift process, but a gradual one that unfolds with understanding and patience.

Chapter 10. Embracing the Future: Evolution of Intergenerational Relationships

Intergenerational relationships have long been an integral part of human societies, playing a crucial role in the transmission of knowledge, traditions, values and skills from one generation to the next. However, with the rapid pace of technological advancement and social change, the nature of these relationships is evolving. Old paradigms are being replaced with new ones, distinct gaps are being bridged, and generational connections are being redefined in powerful, meaningful ways.

10.1. The Traditional Paradigm and Emerging Shifts

Historically, intergenerational relationships have had a traditional structure, often with respect to familial roles and responsibilities. The older generation, possessing the lion's share of knowledge and experience, acted as the primary guide and mentor to the younger generation. The younger ones, on the other hand, were predominantly receptors, absorbing values, wisdom and crafts from their predecessors.

This subservience pattern, however, is being upturned. The paradigm is shifting towards mutuality, where both the young and the old are recognizing the unique values that the other brings to the table. Not only are the elderly passing down traditions now, but the younger generation is also increasingly teaching their seniors, especially around technology, progressive values, and more.

10.2. The Role of Technology

The advent of technology has undeniably played a significant role in this evolving dynamic of intergenerational relationships. It might have once been seen as a barrier, an alienating force between elder technophobes and young technophiles. However, the narrative is changing. We are witnessing an increase in senior netizens and, parallely, the rise of techno-teaching, where the younger generation is grassroots-mentoring the old into the age of technology. This exchange not only helps bridge the digital divide but also fosters mutual respect and understanding.

10.3. Mindful Engagement Across Generations

Mindfulness, the practice of being present and cognizant of our surroundings and experiences, is another potent tool in fostering deep intergenerational connections. By encouraging conversation, attentive listening, and empathetic understanding, mindfulness can help both generations acknowledge and appreciate each other's perspectives.

Practicing mindfulness during these interactions can reveal shared passions, struggles, and hopes that underlie the surface-level differences between generations. The result is a richer, more nuanced understanding of one another, leading to stronger connections and a shared narrative that can transcend generational gaps.

10.4. Changing Social and Economic Landscapes

The evolution of the economy and cultural landscapes also cannot be ignored when considering the shift in intergenerational relationships. Increasingly, there is a move away from the nuclear family model towards multi-generational living. Economically, it makes more sense for generations to live under one roof. It provides opportunities for tighter bonds, shared responsibilities and mutual support systems to thrive.

The social landscape is changing too. With more emphasis on inclusivity and diversity, various generations are stepping into a shared space, tying cultures and traditions together, and creating a beautiful mosaic of shared wisdom and experiences.

10.5. Future Trends and Opportunities

Looking ahead, there is a lot of optimism and vast potential for cultivating even stronger intergenerational relationships. Futuristic trends - such as virtual reality and the proliferation of user-friendly mobile technologies - offer endless opportunities for both generations to share and gain knowledge in new, interactive ways.

Organizations, institutions, and policy-makers can make the most of these trends by endorsing efforts to bridge the generational gap. From introducing policies that encourage intergenerational discourse to developing technologies that appeal to all generations, there is infinitely more to be done.

In all, the future of intergenerational relationships seem promising and vibrant. As the old adage goes, "every old person has a young person inside them, and every young person will become old." Recognizing the commonalities across these life stages, seeing past the differences and evolving together, can enable meaningful and profound connections, creating harmony, empathy, and understanding for generations to come.

Indeed, while intergenerational relationships are changing, their fundamental importance remains - connecting us to our past, grounding us in the present, and propelling us towards a more interconnected future.

Chapter 11. Roadmap For Harmony: Action Steps for building Mindful Intergenerational Connections

Building intergenerational connections steeped in mindfulness can be an incredibly rewarding endeavor. Deep and purposeful links formed between different generations enable shared narratives, unlock empathy, and enable mutual understanding. This chapter outlines a step-by-step guide to constructing such relationships – a roadmap that leads toward harmony.

=== Step 1: Understanding Intergenerational Dynamics

Understanding the dynamics between different generations is crucial. Prioritize gaining knowledge about what shapes each generation and makes them unique – their values, the world events that shaped them, their behaviors, and communication styles. Research indicates that generational traits, while not universally applicable, offer valuable insights into the commonalities within specific age groups, which can aid in creating fruitful connections.

Explore the defining traits of each generation (Boomers, Gen X, Millennials, or Gen Z) and strive to understand their perspectives. Mindfulness in this context means recognizing and respecting the experiences that have shaped these generations. It's about creating a space where all generations can communicate their experiences without judgment, fostering a sense of shared understanding.

=== Step 2: Developing Empathy

With understanding comes empathy. By truly immersing ourselves in the lived experiences of other generations, we can develop a sense of empathy for their challenges, triumphs, and unique experiences. And it is in empathy that harmony and connection truly start to flourish.

Take time to listen to others' first-hand accounts of their respective eras. This will not only foster a sense of shared history but also deepen your individual capacity for empathy. Encourage each generation to share their stories, which can serve as valuable teaching tools. Use meditation and mindfulness techniques to fully present during these interactions, further nurturing an empathetic mindset.

=== Step 3: Encourage Participation in Shared Activities

Shared experiences form the foundation of any strong relationship. Regularly engage in activities that appeal to all generations involved. These shared endeavors, be they common projects, hobbies, or traditions, will serve as a common ground, fostering mutual respect and understanding.

Organize activities that amalgamate the interests of different generations. These could range from games and cooking sessions, to collaborative community projects. Mindful inclusion of everyone's interests often results in a richer, more diverse set of experiences, promoting strong bonds between generations.

=== Step 4: Mindful Communication

Open, sincere, and respectful communication forms the underpinning of any robust connection. Ensure communication is mindful, taking into account the preferred communication styles across different generations. This includes the medium (face-to-face, phone call, emails, text message, etc.), as well as the tone and content of the communication. The aim should be to speak and listen with consideration, openness, and empathy.

Establish norms for communication that honor everyone's needs and preferences, and make changes as needed. Mindfulness, when applied to communication, engenders a productive and rewarding exchange of ideas, fostering shared understanding and connection.

=== Step 5: Cultivating Continued Learning and Adaptation

Finally, it's crucial to remember that building intergenerational connections is not a static process. As with any relationship, it will evolve over time — and that's a good thing. Adaptability and continued learning are essential.

Commit to ongoing education about other generations' experiences, even (especially) when they differ from your own. Engage in discussions and activities that challenge your views and promote growth. Keep up-to-date with new findings and research in the field of intergenerational dynamics to keep your approach fresh and informed.

By continually learning and adapting, you'll ensure that your approach to building and maintaining these precious connections stays dynamic, inclusive, and impactful.

Remember, the adventure of intergenerational connection is one of mutual growth and shared understanding. While it may be challenging at times, the rewards — empathy, shared narratives, deeper relationships — are plentiful. Armed with this roadmap, you're ready to embark on this enriching journey. Let's bridge that gap together.